What <u>Kids</u> Are Saying A

"My favorite part of this book was Officer Leo's Dad-Jokes. This is the BEST BOOK EVER!"

-Alexander
12 years old

"I like the part where Officer Leo talks about helping kids. Because bullies are bad"

-Carmelo
7 years old

Officer Leo Pickle's

"My favorite part is the way Officer Leo describes his job"

-Liz
11 years old

"I never knew my SRO like I know him now. I mean, I knew him... but I didn't KNOW him. He's nice"

-Patricia
9 years old

"SUPER-DUPER"
School Resource Adventure

This book belongs to a "SUPER-DUPER" kid named:

_____

Write your name on this line

More feedback at www.OfficerLeoPickle.com

What **Adults** Are Saying About...

Officer Leo Pickle's
"SUPER-DUPER"
School Resource Adventure

"This was well-written with a sound intent to improve student relationships with School Resource Officers. The book does a tremendous job communicating the importance of School Resource Officers and how they keep us all safe. Job well done. I enjoyed the balance of humor and real connections to School Resource officers and students. I will definitely purchase a copy for my own children and other copies for my building"

- Bradley Lehman
Principal

"Loved the jokes at the bottom of the pages – funny and clever! Loved the layout and easy to read content. This book would be a great addition to any school library"

- Marta Almiron
Kindergarten Teacher

On a scale of 1-10 how would you rate this book?

"I give this book a 10"

- Gerald Earley
Assistant Principal

What was your favorite part of this book?

"The idea, what a great idea. Kids need this information"

Is this a book you would read to your own children or students?

"Yes!"

- Adrian Ocampo
School District Executive Director

"This book is an excellent resource that allows teachers to introduce the integrated role of a School Resource Officer. The "dad" jokes made the book fun and enjoyable. The activities on the last pages were a fun way to interact with students"

- Maritza Peña
Personnel Administrative Manager
New York City Police Department

More feedback at www.OfficerLeoPickle.com

Copyright © 2020 Milton A. Rosario

ISBN: 978-1-7360228-0-1

All rights reserved. No part of this publication may be reproduced, stored in a retrieval system, or transmitted, in any form or by any means, electronic, mechanical, photocopying, recording, or otherwise, without the author's prior written permission. Requests for permission to photocopy or replicate, in any fashion, any portion of this book for any use should be directed to the publisher at the address below:

Published by:

Rosario Publishing
P.O. Box 732
Vero Beach, FL 32961

Made in the United States of America.

This book is dedicated to my parents, Anibal and Felicia,
who have taught me unconditional love
and to my two amazing children, Megan and Nicholas,
through whom I have the honor and privilege of practicing my parents' teachings.

Hello everyone! My name is Milton Rosario. I am a School Resource Officer. That means I am a police officer that works at a school. I am an employee of our local sheriff's office. But I report to the school I am assigned to, every day the school is open, and work there all day long.

I bet you have a School Resource Officer at the school you attend. Do you know him or her? Do you know what they do? Do you know how they can help you? Not many kids do. If you don't, don't worry, you and I are going to change that **TODAY**! We're going on an adventure!

Section One
"The Adventure"

In this book, I'll be showing you what we School Resource Officers do and how we can help you in <u>and</u> out of school. To do this, however, I will need to transform into my alter ego, **"OFFICER LEO PICKLE."** Officer Pickle is a School Resource Officer in my favorite make-believe town, Pickleville, U.S.A. He works at Pickleville Elementary School.

Are you ready for the transformation? Let's go! Oh, wait... there's one thing you should know about Officer Pickle, or "Officer Leo", as the kids call him. Officer Leo **<u>LOVES</u>** dad-jokes. So, at the bottom of every page in this adventure section, Officer Leo will provide you with one of his favorite dad-jokes. Let's read the first dad-joke now.

What happens when a School Resource Officer goes to bed at night? He goes "under**<u>COVER</u>**"!

"The Transformation"

Let's transform now and go to school. Ready? Let's go!!!

What do you say when you get a pickle for FREE?
What a great "**DILL**"! (*deal*)

Okay, now that I transformed into Officer Leo, let's fly over to Pickleville Elementary and have a look around.

What do you call a flying School Resource Officer?

A "heli-**COPPER**"!!!

"Protectors"

Most schools have School Resource Officers. They do many things on campus. One of the things School Resource Officers do is keep kids and teachers safe from bad people outside the school campus. This way, teachers can teach, and kids can learn in a safe environment. School Resource Officers are your friends and protectors. They are trusted adults.

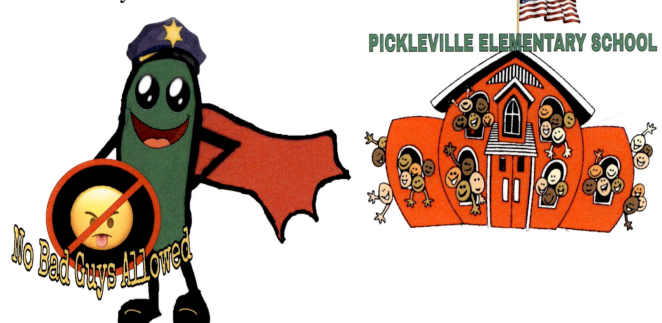

Which dinosaur makes the best School Resource Officer?

"A Tricera-**COPS**"

"Protectors"

School Resource Officers can protect you from fellow students. For example, if a fellow student tries to bother or bully you, the School Resource Officer can intervene. They can also help you if **ANYONE - ANYWHERE**, is trying to hurt you in **ANY** other way.

What four letters does a School Resource Officer know

that frightens bullies?

"O.I.C.U.!"

"Lay Counselors"

School Resource Officers are good listeners. Many of us, like myself, have pretty big ears and an even bigger heart. We can listen and give you good advice if you are ever sad, anxious, or worried about anything. If you feel like you have a ginormous problem or merely a small problem, we can help. No problem is ever too big or too small for your School Resource Officer. You and your School Resource Officer have something in common; you were both your age once.

What's the most depressing day for chickens?

"**FRY**-day!"

"Teachers"

School Resource Officers sometimes teach kids about laws, driver safety, and other civics related classes. Some of these classes are during the regular school day, and some may take place after the regular school day is over - kind of like after-school sports. Some School Resource Officers, like myself, are former teachers. Others have many years of experience that help them teach. But, we all have one thing in common, we love our students and want nothing but the best for them.

Why do School Resource Officers teach law

and don't coach swimming class?

They know the law, but they'd constantly have to stop to

"test the waters" if they coached swimming.

"First Aid Providers"

Most School Resource Officers have been trained in first-aid. They can help you if you're sick or if you get injured in any way. School Resource Officers can also help teachers, administrators, and other school staff if they get hurt or injured. School Resource Officers are part of the "9-1-1" emergency communication system and can radio their paramedic friends if they need to. Then, the paramedics can come to the school with lights and sirens in a big shiny ambulance.

What do you call first aid on a pirate ship?

Sea-P-Yaaaaaaaaarrr!!!! (C.P.R.)

"Trusted Friend"

In addition to their regular everyday school functions, many School Resource Officers coach baseball, football, basketball, or other sports at their school. Sometimes, School Resource Officers are involved in school-based events like lunch-with-a-cop, bike-giveaways, or bike-rodeos. Other School Resource Officers, like myself, regularly visit kids that are hospital-bound in pediatric wards to cheer them up. School Resource Officers LOVE to spend time with their students.

Knock, knock. Who's there? Police. Police who?

"Police" hurry and open the gym door

so I can come in and play with you guys!

"Community Members"

School Resource Officers are members of our communities. Many of us have kids that attend the same school you attend. We love seeing our students and their parents around town while we shop at the local supermarket or while we walk around with our families. If you see your School Resource Officer around town, please feel free to say hello to them.

Why did the School Resource Officer rush to the little league game?
　　　　　He heard somebody **"stole"** second base!

"Recap"

Let's quickly go over what we learned before we go on to the next section. Name some of the things School Resource Officers do around your school.

1. _____

2. _____

3. _____

4. _____

5. _____

6. _____

What's an astronaut's favorite part of a computer?

The "**Space**" bar!

Section Two
INTERACTIVE ACTIVITY

"Getting-to-Know-You Exercises"

On the following pages I have provided you with guided questions that will help you and your School Resource Officer get to know each other better. If your School Resource Officer is leading the reading of this book, see how many of these guided questions you and your School Resource Officer can answer now. You'll see how similar you and your School Resource Officer are.

If you're reading this book with anyone other than your School Resource Officer, ask them to deliver the questions to your School Resource Officer. You can pen-pal your way through this exercise using some old-fashioned back and forth written communication.

Getting to know your School Resource Officer is very important. This way, you will always know where you can go for help from your new trusted friend. Or, in my case, know where you can go for a good dad-joke.

"The Guessing Game"

Students, try to guess what your School Resource Officer's answer will be about himself/herself: (this can be a written activity or a hand-raising discussion activity)

I think my School Resource Officer's favorite hobby is: _____

I think my School Resource Officer's favorite sport is: _____

I think my School Resource Officer's favorite color is: _____

I think my School Resource Officer's favorite ice-cream is: _____

I think my School Resource Officer's favorite food is: _____

I think my School Resource Officer's favorite dream car would be: _____

I think my School Resource Officer's favorite pet is: _____

I think my School Resource Officer's favorite person in the world is: _____

I think the person my School Resource Officer looks up to the most is: _____

When my School Resource Officer was my age, I think he/she wanted to grow up and work as a: _____

I think my School Resource Officer's least favorite food is: _____

I think my School Resource Officer's favorite thing about school is: _____

I think if my School Resource Officer could have a super power he/she would want it to be: _____

I think when my School Resource Officer was in school his/her favorite gym game was: _____

I think if my School Resource Officer could have his/her own country it would be called: _____

I think if my School Resource Officer could have three wishes the FIRST one would be: _____

I think if my School Resource Officer could have three wishes the SECOND one would be: _____

I think if my School Resource Officer could have three wishes the THIRD one would be: _____

For your personal information:

My Guidance Counselor's name is: _____

My Guidance Counselor's office is located in: _____

My Dean's name is: _____

My Dean's office is located in: _____

My School Resource Officer's name is: _____

My School Resource Officer's office is located in: _____

My School Resource Officer's office telephone number is: _____

My School Resource Officer's email address is: _____

In case of **emergency** you can always call **9-1-1**

Notes:

Notes:

Notes:

Made in the USA
Monee, IL
03 May 2022